RECEIPT OF DAYS

RECEIPT OF DAYS

Thomas Fasano

Coyote Canyon Press
Claremont, California

Copyright © 2025 by Thomas Fasano

All rights reserved.

No part of this publication may be reproduced, distributed, or transmitted in any form or by any means, including photocopying, recording, or other electronic or mechanical methods, without the prior written permission of the author, except in the case of brief quotations embodied in critical reviews and certain other noncommercial uses permitted by copyright law.

First Edition

Table of Contents

Tapestry of Thought 1
Temporal Imprints 7
Ephemeral Weights 11
Indifferent Continuums 15
Temporal Witness 20
Cloud-Scape Clarity 25
Morning's Unruly Thoughts 30
Serif Conspiracies 35
Seasonal Alchemy 39
Weathered Thoughts 45
Frostbound Musings 50
Tapestry of Contrasts 56
Winter's Script 60
Solstice Shadows 65
Temporal Whispers 70
Contrast in Spoonfuls 76
Cyclic Bonds 81
Internal Fireworks 87
Shadow's Whisper 92
Predatory Melodies 97
Temporal Continuance 101
Temporal Threshold 105
Indifferent Light 111
Temporal Dichotomy 116
Transmutation Harmonies 122
Sunlight on Feathers 127
Boundary Currents 131
Rain's Philosophy 135
Condensation's Philosophy 140
Linguistic Topography 146
Eternal Cycles 152

Tapestry of Thought

The roll unfurls: an
endless white cascade,
   the muse's challenge
etched in thinness, space
demanding brevity, yet
depth: an odd dichotomy.

Each tap of keys, a small
victory in rhythm, the
  type-bars striking ribbon
to tape: a bond formed in
constraint.

Could these lines bridge
the infinite, carve
clarity from a stream of
consciousness, narrow as
the tape itself, yet vast
as the sky's own reach?

The mountain speaks of
pressure, gravity–forces
that mold its peaks and
  feed the streams that
trickle, bleed into
rivers below.

Here, at my desk, the
tape's length mirrors
thought, uncertain in
breadth, uncertain in
direction: a path cleared
by persistence.

This thin strip captures
   echoes of my musings, the
muse whispering of
endurance, the natural
flow from mind to matter.

   Light dances on the
  surface of water:
reflective, refractive.
It is the poet's medium:
light, water, word—all
flowing alike.

   Each character punctuates
the physical strain, the
   metaphor of back pain:
how much weight can one
slender strip hold?

The muse, she is water:
   cooling, flowing,
    essential, yet how she
erodes the poet's
resolve, with relentless,
shaping hands.

Can I sing a song here,
   on this ribbon of paper,
  that remains unforgotten,
or will it curl, fade, a
   relic of attempted
permanence?

    This experiment— a form
both liberated and
confined, informs each
letter I strike, a
paradox of creative
   spirit.

Through my window, the
season shifts, unnoticed,
from dew-laden mornings
to frost's silent siege:
transformation without
witness.

   But the tape sees, hears,
     absorbs the shifts within
     and without, logging the
subtleties of days: a
diary, a chronicle,
   bound.

   Poetry, a force of
nature, like the
 mountains to the clouds,
flows downward, fills
 basins, escapes into
oceans of thought,
uncontainable, yet
directed.

  Today, I fold patience
into my craft, bending
like the willow, roots
deep, branches tender,

    swayed by gales, yet
unbroken.

The muse, relentless,
    asks: "Will you endure,
poet? Can your back bear
  the burden of lines, the
weight of water, the
    depth of thought?"

  My answer lies in
continuation, in the
  unspooling roll, the
persistent clatter of old
keys, the forming of
worlds, thin yet infinite
on my desk.

    Silence follows each
question, the muse
    pausing, thoughtful: her
test is not of words
alone, but of will, of
the capacity to harness
the torrent within.

Leaf by leaf, the seasons
turn, pages of nature's
own book, and I, a humble
scrivener, seek to
emulate this manuscript,
authored by a grander
hand.

The tape is a river, I am
its reluctant ferryman,
    guiding words across the
    currents of thought to
banks unseen, unknown.

    Each stroke is a paddle
dipped, each line a
current crossed, and the
journey, oh the journey—
it is long, filled with
    both dread and wonder,
uncertainty and awe.

As night encroaches, the
artificial lamplight
becomes my sun,
    illuminating the path
laid out on paper, each
line a step into the
        dark.

The muse, capricious,
offers no torch, no
    guide, save the
     relentless push of water,
  of creativity, that flows
from mountains of the
mind.

I question the quixotic
quest, the folly of
mapping thoughts on tape
too narrow for the

landscape it must chart:
an endeavor doomed, or
  destined?

Yet with each line, a
resolution, a quiet
rebellion against the
    finite, a stretching
towards the infinite
within the limits—

And so the roll unfurls,
  word by word,
its edges never quite meeting,
thoughts pressed into thinness,
leaving their trace.

Temporal Imprints

In the quiet of morning:
the typewriter silent, a
quiet indictment: my
yesterday's words, too
neat, too aligned.

I stare, doubting: should
    lines mirror the tangled
roots: or strive for
    clarity, like a stream
cut through ice?

Glaciers inch forward:
indifferent to the span
   of a human heart, erasing
  histories as they carve
  valleys.

 Troy fell in smoke, and
Sumerians drowned under
silent sands— all that
endeavor, lost to time's
sweep.

Our lives, mere blinks:
in the long stare of a
volcanic mount, molten
    rock beneath presses up,
     reshapes continents.

I think of Odysseus,
leader flawed by hubris,
each choice a ripple
across wine-dark seas:
his purpose questioned.

Am I, too, adrift on this
sea of words? This
journey of ink— does it
    matter, or is it just
self-indulgence?

I type, erase, pause: the
    sheet blank again, like a
field of snow, waiting
  for footprints to mark
the way forward.

    Should my verses stand as
      monuments or dust?
Imitate the chaos of
    nature, or offer a beacon
through fog?

Visions of epochs where
    glaciers retreat, and new
    islands rise, flood my
  thoughts— the relentless
push of earth.

    History whispers of
empires like waves,
rising, then pulled back

into the deep, forgotten,
    unmoored.

Tides of doubt pull, and
I am caught, my words a
    frail bark on the swell
of ages, seeking a
    distant shore.

Is there a shore?
Odysseus too sought:
home, a fixed point in a
   shifting world— his
     journey fraught.

 I type again: words not
as stones, but as leaves,
 carried by a stream, ever
changing, ever flown.

The day wanes; shadows
grow long: my room a
cavern where thoughts
    echo, murmur, then fade.

 I gaze outside: the sky a
canvas of twilight hues,
pondering if darkness
holds its own truths.

  Does the night reveal or
  conceal? Stars peek,
silent: ancient light

traveling through vast,
   indifferent space.

   My typewriter— an altar
of sorts, where I
sacrifice these fleeting
thoughts, hoping they
   resonate.

Odysseus faced monsters,
I confront the blank
page, both seeking a
   form, a story to fill the
      expanse of days.

Night settles in,
quietly, like snow: each
flake a poem, a soft
   descent into the unknown.

Finally, I understand:
the journey is both:
clarity and chaos,
darkness and light, all
      woven tight.

So I write, embracing the
complex dance: my words
not the end, but a path
   through shadows, towards
dawn's light.

Ephemeral Weights

    Yesterday's gray bird:
gone, like a whisper in
    the windy: how much can
absence weigh? More, I
think, than presence: an
echo fills the hollows,
more than a song ever
did.

A leaf, brittle with
winter's kiss, clings to
the branch: it is not
green, not alive, but
    holding on: a testament
to the now, and yet, so
transient.

What should I make of
  this, the missing bird,
  the persistent leaf?
  Should I see a sign, a
    metaphor for our own,
brief stutters on the
earth?

    Do these moments, small
and delicate as the bones
in a bird's wing, carry
the weight of the
eternal, or are they just
light, gone when the wind
shifts?

    I walk, boots crunching
     the frozen crust of snow,
   a bridle path stretched
like a promise beneath
the sprawling arms of
bare trees: each breath I
  take is a taking in of
the world, so filled with
the minute and the
mighty.

A yellow horse-turd,
steaming in the cold:
   absurd, and yet how
grounding, reminding me
    that life, in all its
  facets, is life:
unavoidable, messy,
vital.

   Why did the elephant wear
red sneakers? To hide in
  the strawberry patch, of
course. Laughter bubbles
  up, irreverent but
necessary: we are serious
creatures, too often
  forgetting that
   silliness, too, roots us
in life, keeps us from
floating away like so
many gray birds.

Evening falls: a curtain,
or perhaps just another
page turning on this day.
    Inside the warm kitchen,
fruitcake spices the air,
amber and earthy, rich
  with nuts and candied
fruit: each bite is a
warm embrace against the
chill.

Outside, the world is
white and still, as if
waiting for something to
fill it: perhaps the bird
will return, or another
 like it, or nothing at
all, and still, the snow
will melt, the earth will
warm, the trees will bud.

Life dances on this edge
    of impermanence, every
moment a potential
goodbye, every day a
   chance to hold on or let
 go: and we, caught in the
middle, wonder at it all,
the slow crawl and sudden
flight, the ordinariness
of bread rising in the
  oven, the marvel of
starlight, a universe
untouchable yet somehow
inside us, too.

What then, of this day,
this path, this missing
bird? Everything,
perhaps, or nothing at
all: what matters is the
seeing, the walking, the
making room for laughter
and for silence, the
warmth of the kitchen and
the cold of the path, the
ephemeral brush of a gray
   wing against the vast,
eternal sky.

Indifferent Continuums

Crash came down: eighty
souls, in sudden rupture:
bound to earth, not by
choice: wind whispers
indifferent through the
    sycamore leaves: while
   fire licks, ferocious, at
the metal bones:

each flame another prayer
   unanswered: or is it
simply nature, following
its cold laws:
probability scattering
dice on a cloud-dense
board:

I stood, far from the
direct hit, my home
 spared by mere degrees: a
twist in the wind's mood,
a flicker in fate's gaze:
is randomness godly, or
god merely random:

those eighty lives, now
whispers, do they mingle
with the ash, the dust
that settles softly on
the leaves, on the
waters, on the
unsuspecting deer

stepping careful through
the quiet:

does the deer consider
    the sky, the possibility
of fire from above, or
does it simply drink its
fill, alert only to the
   rustle of predation:

I reckon not tragedy, but
the execution of
  existence, each creature
enacting its survival,
  unaware of the stories
dying above, in the
heavens:

so to speak of spirits
   ascending, of bodies
broken by gravity's pull,
is to speak in human
terms, granting flame a
   sanctity, turning smoke
into spirit:

yet the universe expands,
   uncaring, focusing not on
these eighty sparks
extinguished, but on the
   endless dark, its cold
     vastness brittle as frost
on grass:

so I walk this narrow
path, where ants march in
their diligent line,
their labor undisturbed
  by sorrow, or the grand
      dramas of humankind:

and I, too, am just a
     passing breath, a mote
floating on the day's
sigh, chasing the
illusion of permanence,
in a world where
permanence replies not,
  does not console, nor
explain why the storm
veers one way, not
  another:

is the ant, then, wiser,
not querying the why, but
building beneath, steady
despite the thunder's
    threat, or the sudden
    shadow of wings above:

  perhaps in this ongoing
flux, this relentless
push of time, where cells
divide and galaxies spin,
    lies the truest prayer,
the real hymn: silence,
    acceptance:

for as the sun falls
today, untroubled by the
   smoke rising, somewhere a
   child still laughs, a dog
barks at a thrown stick,
life insists:

therefore, what is left
but to observe, to learn
humility from grass, that
bows to wind and rises,
to find in the molecular
dance some hint of
eternity's rhythm:

if fire destroys, it also
   cleanses, and in the
charred soil, new seeds
   find a fierce blessing, a
     chance to root deeply
    where once stood another
forest:

 thus, do we stand not
apart, but as part of
this grand, indifferent
cycle, love and loss but
particles in the vast
sweep of existence: each
human heart, a world,
    each ending, a beginning:

and if this seems a
meager comfort, look to
the stars, old light
touching us from a past
    beyond our reach, each
       photon a story, a journey
    of immense solitude:

thus, in contemplating
  the vast, I find a
strange peace, not in
understanding, but in
being with the leaf, the
ant, the falling star:
all bound by the same
     unyielding rules, playing
out the infinite game,
unaware of the count,
unswayed by the tally of
grief or joy:

so when the news speaks
of tragedy, of lives
snuffed into silence: I
  think of that deer, still
drinking, unaware: how
    Earth holds both our
stories and our silence,
  neither more weighted
than the other in time's
    vast equation, where
each breath, each death,
    dissolves into the same
    infinite indifference.

Temporal Witness

The morning fumbles
   forward: a pale sun
    pierces sumac branches—
buried deep in red glory:
  but the light, hesitant,
asks permission to
    proceed.

Bluejay lands: a flash of
certainty amid the
wavering branches— its
sharp eye: a mirror
collecting fragments of a
scattered dawn.

  This perch: temporary, as
    all things with wings or
      thoughts, or light that
dances between leaves: it
moves, it must move, or
perish.

  I watch: poet, or
observer, or merely
another transient figure
 in this shifting scene—
words form in my mind
like frost on grass:
    delicate yet somehow
invasive.

Can I claim creation, or
    am I just echoing the
whispers of wind, the arc
  of the bird's flight, the
twist of the sumac as it
    reaches for sparse
warmth?

  A child writes on paper:
about feelings, not
crafted poems: her words
    flow like
    streams—unforced, rich
with the debris of
  unfiltered truth.

Is this not closer to
poetry than my labored
    lines, seeking to encase
a moment in amber, when
it longs to live, to
   pulse, to escape?

  The sky balances on the
    cusp of winter: its mood,
uncertain, like my own
role in this script of
seasons— how will winter
    come?

Will it crash upon us
    with the force of a
storm, or seep into our
bones like a slow chill,

whispering through the
seams of the world?

A bluejay scatters this
reflection— its
    departure: as sudden as
its arrival, a reminder
that everything is in
motion, even silence.

  And below, starlings
create their own chaos,
    intricate patterns that
defy simple tracing, like
  thoughts that refuse to
align neatly on paper.

I am caught in between:
    the simplicity of a blue
moment and the noise of
competing needs, the
straightforward line and
    the mesh of connections
that form each breath.

  As the sun climbs,
  hesitation burns away,
leaving behind the
certainty of day, even if
    that certainty is only
that light will fade.

All is in flux: even this
grove, even the staunch
sumac, or the trajectory
of a single, darting
bird— and am I not the
same, a creature of
phases and tides?

Creation or imitation:
perhaps these are just
  terms we use to soothe
our need for significance
in the grandeur or the
decay.

Yet in the cold clarity
   of morning, with every
  leaf and feather defined
against a waking sky, I
feel the pull— to write,
to witness, to be.

   This day unfolds as I set
words down, knowing they
might not capture, might
    not hold—yet still they
strive, and so do I.

Each line proclaims its
frail attempt to bridge
the vast between thought
and the language that
   bears it, a cumbersome
   yet hopeful craft.

And in this moment, with
frost still claiming each
blade of grass, a clarity
   emerges— not of answers,
but of the act of
   seeking.

For what are we but
searchers, in landscapes
   internal and external:
   seeking to understand, or
at least to stand under
   the weight of our own
questions?

   Thus, the day decides:
not just the weather, but
the shape of thoughts,
the rhythm of emotions—
it lays down a path with
light, and shadow, and
pause.

The sumac, silent now,
   holds droplets
of morning's revelation:
each bead a lens where
   dawn and dusk merge,
where watching becomes
   being, and being
dissolves into the vast
  morning song.

Cloud-Scape Clarity

Clouds gather, then
    disband: such is the sky,
    like my mind on uncertain
   days, fluttering: serene:
then shadowed:

Oh, Muse, today I need
your light—shine through
    this varied cloud-scape
of thought, guide my
scattered senses:

In fields wide and
   splayed beneath this
indecisive sky, birds dip
and arc— symbols of my
     faltering clarity?

Perhaps their flight is
   effortless: or is it a
frantic beating against
the vast, enveloping air?
Unclear I am, as they
seem clear:

These bursts of sun,
these stretches of gray—
why must they tease so,
like a lover undecided,
   or a heart half-open,
half-closed?

The light changes: so
    does my heart: partly
sunny, mostly lost, I
plead: reveal, reveal!
Yet fear my worthiness of
revelation:

How do I sustain such a
pursuit, this endless
  crafting of words, when
    each thought feels as
fleeting as a cloud's
shadow?

    Time passes: perhaps like
the erosion of rock,
slow, almost unseen,
until the landscape is
    utterly transformed:

And about this missing
bird— that absence
speaks, doesn't it? like
a love unreturned, or a
    thought unthought:

An airplane crosses
above, briefly, a stark,
sure line against the
  uncertainty of
cloud-soaked heavens:
will it too fall,
  disappear into the
unseen?

Should my words mimic
nature's chaos or strive
for some semblance of
order? The heart yearns
for a pattern, and yet
the soul delights in
surprise:

This tension, this
   interplay of light and
dark, clarity and
complexity, spiritual
longing versus the
visceral, pulling ground:

I am caught between
realms, seeking signs in
     randomness, wondering if
fate directs us or if we
   arrange the stars
   ourselves:

Muse, am I a vessel for
divine breath or merely a
voice howling in the
   void? Is any love real,
or is each one just an
     ideal, shadowed in
half-light?

Across the turbulent sky,
my thoughts
fly—tentative, beginning
and then breaking,

seeking form amid
formlessness:

Endurance is my quiet
   rebellion against the
     impermanence of now, the
   bird that returns, the
cloud that dissipates:

There is beauty, perhaps,
in this struggle to
articulate, in the
  ever-shifting line
between what is said and
what is meant:

Amidst these
accumulations of cloud,
there are gaps, bright
and sudden, where the sun
pours through: so, too,
my Muse, might clarity
   come:

Finally, as light dims to
    dusk, and clouds claim
their victory, I accept
the interplay, the
inseparable dance of
light and dark:

With each line, I seek
balance between revealing
and concealing, between
 the known path and the
shadowed, mysterious one:

Oh, Muse, in this
 fleeting light, grant me
  a glimpse of truth, let
me grasp it, briefly,
 before night comes,
unambiguous, dark:

Still, the chase is not
 in vain: for in the
pursuit, in the question,
 lies the essence of all
poetry, the trembling
  heart of all love.

Morning's Unruly Thoughts

Misty gray cloaks the
dawn: a veil that softens
the hard edges of night,
yet my mind races, sharp,
unbidden.

    Restlessness seethes, a
kettle left to whistle
its high, piercing note.
Stirred: thoughts like
leaves in a gusty wind.

Outside, the world holds
its breath in mist, while
inside, my world teems
    with the unseen flow of
  blood, of ideas.

  Curious, to upset the
morning's quiet: might I
scatter birds as one
scatters thoughts,
unruly?

Each wingbeat, a
punctuation in the thick
silence— their departure
a thing of beauty, of
chaos birthed from my
impulse.

Yet the impulse leads
back, always, to
   stillness: the
after-wind, settling.

Floors creak under weight
of unnoticed life: my
   wife descends, intent on
routine, grace in her
steps.

Dishes clatter, a
   comforting percussion in
the monotone day. She
does not see the shadows
I wrestle.

The adding-machine tape
whirs, a relentless
creed: I tally words,
scores in a poet's game
of endless seeking.

Is it worth it? — this
incessant scribing, these
lines that stretch,
   writhing, trying to catch
the uncatchable?

   Doubt nibbles at the
edges of creation, a
mouse in the pantry of my
resolve. Yet, I feed it

scraps, unsure if it's
friend or foe.

Family voices rise: a
   clash, a storm of words.
We are ephemeral as mist,
yet hard as the rock
beneath.

Pain is a teacher, sharp
and precise, cutting
through fog, a clarity in
    the confusion.

The post office beckons,
a walk through damp;
    envelopes and stamps,
   simple transactions that
ground me.

   Back home, the silence is
   a different shade:
   thicker, as if colored by
   our voices, spoken
earlier.

Artistic fatigue— a well
run dry, yet from its
depths, sometimes, a
seep: a surprising
    spring.

Why this obsession with
　writing, with measuring
my life in lineated
breaths against cold
paper?

Each poem, a tiny act of
　rebellion against the
finitude of days, against
the certainty of ends.

I sit, the tape before
me, a spool of potential:
　　how many more lines will
emerge before the final
silence?

Restoration through
words, a paradox of
　emptying and filling,
　each line a step back
toward the fullness.

　　Gray mornings mirror my
spirit, yet also feed it:
　there is beauty in this
soft, diffused light, in
　the hush.

Words, like mist, gather:
　　not quite rain, not yet
river, but water all the
　　same, sustaining,
　　　life-giving.

My mind winds down, a
clock unwound, and in the
stillness, I find,
strangely, movement:
continuous, inescapable,
like the earth's turning,
like the heart's beating.

   Birds, perhaps startled
by a soundless call,
return. They settle into
their places, as do I,
into mine.

Serif Conspiracies

In my hands, the thin
spine: freshly inked,
cold, a slice of my
musings, bound, sold, yet
 oddly foreign: like
 finding a photo where you
don't recognize yourself,
 smiling with strangers.

 A little flip through:
 pages whispering their
 crisp approval, or is it
mockery? Imposter's
laughter, hiding in serif
fonts, a conspiracy of
paper and ink.

 I shuffle the book back
into its cardboard
cocoon, addressed to me,
but perhaps it's a cosmic
error: meant for someone
more deserving of these
 bound ideas.

Outside, the city holds
its breath in the chill,
 December's grip
tightening. We're to buy
gifts, not thoughts
 today: the practical
exchange of cash for joy,

a ledger balanced by
cheerful LEDs.

    Marshalls bustles, a
symphony of commerce:
  shelves lined with
everything one doesn't
need but might desire.
Here I am, a book
birther, lost among
    gadgets and plastic
garlands.

"Tinsel and truth," I
mutter, to no one in
particular, each
reflecting light in
   glossy deception. Wife,
     pragmatic, unearths
   bargains like rare earth
metals, precious in their
    ordinariness.

The checkout lines snake,
   an ouroboros of
     consumption. My book, in
my pocket, feels
  insignificant, a leaf
caught in a tornado of
receipts and wrapping.

    On to dinner at Mac's,
the local beacon of fried
fare. Here, existence

simmers down to the
essence: eating, talking,
   living while the globe
spins unperturbed by my
   literary advent.

Fork clinks softly, salad
leaves sigh under
dressing— a mundane
symphony. I muse out
loud, "Wrote a book, but
lost to lettuce in the
   grandeur war."

Wife chuckles, calls it a
draw: "Your words might
outlive the lettuce."

  Then, whimsically to
Oroville, where books
   lie stacked, casual
     sediments of thought.
   Aristophanes— I lift his
weight, hoping to steal
some ancient wit.

His plays dance with
political bite and human
folly, a mirror to my own
    endeavors, where humor
     masks the tremble of
truth, delicate as frost
on glass.

Back home, the book
awaits me, unblinking. I
   realize it's not the
   volume but the echo it
leaves that frets me, and
   maybe that's okay: books
   are seeds, not stone
monuments.

In our bed, we laugh: at
  the day, at my fears, at
how small things loom
    large until seen from the
    distance of shared
comfort, a quiet room,
windows looking out over
    a world that does not
pause for poets or their
ponderings.

I drift to sleep, book by
   my side, a tethered
balloon, held close, let
go: achievements and
   doubts like paired wings—
necessary for the flight
through the human night.

Seasonal Alchemy

rain taps the window: is
it knocking for entry, or
merely keeping rhythmic
company with my quiet,
indoor thoughts?

the texture shifts:
flakes begin to edge out
the rain: fine lines to
　softer sweeps of white,
now accumulating.

snow falls: each flake,
an architect of silence,
muting the customary
sounds: a world redrawn
underneath a hushed
blanket.

　　this transformation,
　　　subtle yet complete, from
liquid motion to solid
stillness: captures the
essence

of change: how gently it
layers over the familiar,
leaving shapes intact but
　altering their spirit and
their substance.

from water to crystal,
the cycle perpetuates
itself: the transmutation
   presupposes no end: the
    indefinite revisited.

  up above, the sky seems
an ancient loom where
clouds weave the fabric
of season: rain to snow,
warm to cold.

below, the ground accepts
   its new garment, a bridal
gown of frost, promising
   a season of concealed
germination.

inside, the heat hums, a
reminder of human craft,
our petty defiance
against the grand designs
  of nature.

but even as I sit
enveloped in warmth, the
cold seeps into my bones,
like a myth creeping into
    reality.

the snow speaks in soft
tongues, whispering old
    tales: of Demeter

mourning the land's
barren slumber.

is it not Persephone lost
to us once more, her
departure marked by the
cold's arrival, her
mother's grief

painting the earth with
frost instead of flowers?
Here the myth finds
residence, in the chill
that settles

deep into the soul.
Transformations led not
by the vigorous
assertions of Zeus, but
by quiet, tireless

Hypnos, god of sleep,
   blanketing the world in
dreams of white, easing
the vibrant into the
monochrome.

do the birds dream of
   their missing colors,
fearing the blank slate
upon which they can no
longer paint their
presence?

or do they, perhaps,
understand better than
we, that beneath the
apparent stasis of winter
lies the deepest change?

that beneath the snow, a
world of intermingled
roots and seeds prepares
for the burst of spring's
vibrant reckoning?

or is winter itself a
    prison, bars made not of
iron, but of ice, each
flake a cold, soft warden
in a vast, frozen
  confinement?

  in the silence, I hear
more than the absence of
 noise: I hear the slow,
   steady pulsing of the
earth, its breath under
   the snow.

the snow falls, and I
imagine it not as a
   cover, but as a cleansing
 wave: purification
  through the alchemy of
cold.

each flake: a soft kiss
upon the land, a touch so
   gentle, it turns weight
into fluff, motion into a
quiet quilt.

from my window, the world
is a canvas, erased and
redrawn with every
falling flake, each one a
thought

from the sky, pondering
heavy matters in the
lightest of forms, the
world transformed not by
force, but by whispering

flakes that settle like
dust in old books, each
layer a page in a story
told by winter's chilled
breath.

  soon, perhaps, I'll tread
outside, to disrupt the
   perfect layer with
footprints, each step a
signature

  on the white parchment:
not to mar but to join
    the winter's writing,

adding my brief marks to
 time's manuscript, each
print a syllable in the
 season's slow verse,
until darkness fills them
 in: nature's editing,
completing the day's
 composition, making all
tracks temporary: sacred
 in their passing.

Weathered Thoughts

Clouds gather like
  thoughts: heavy weather:
a metaphor for the mind's
burden.

  The road to York twists:
  each curve a folded
secret, my poem beside
me.

    The paper crackles, a
    delicate life housed in
my grip: thin as breath.

How I cling to it: words
that might scatter like
    ash in one cruel gust.

The engine hums low, a
backdrop to my musings,
its rhythm constant.

Life outside speeds by,
  indifferent to the pages
that shape my quiet fear.

I turn off the route: a
brief stop at my cousin's
house, bright with
laughter.

Their chatter brushes
against the silence of my
guarded manuscript.

To them, it's just paper,
not the fragile vessel of
my soul's quiet scream.

A child's balloon pops:
startlingly ephemeral, a
burst then gone.

 Thus, my work could fade:
lost to fire or
forgetfulness,
   unremarked, unmourned.

   Back on the road, dusk
bleeds into the horizon,
  dyeing it with loss.

   York unfolds in layers, a
mix of old haunts and the
pulse of the new.

Each street corner a
crossroad between past
     and what comes:
unforgiving.

Yet, the roll of words
sits patient, an
unassuming companion,
waiting.

For what? Preservation?
Or the fated unraveling
   that haunts each
creation?

A stoplight blinks red: a
command to halt, to
   breathe, to fear, and to
      hope.

With every mile, a line
is drawn: between here
and home, now and then,
   lost—

 and found. My hands
tighten around the wheel:
steering through the
   landscape of thought.

   Night's curtain descends:
     veiling the world in
  shadows, thick with
unknowns.

But the paper's pulse—
    heartbeat of penned
 musings— feels louder in
the hush.

I navigate through
memory's terrain, each
   turn a stanza, reshaped.

   The journey and the
destination blur: what
   matters is the motion,
the act—

   of writing, of moving, of
fearing, yet daring to
sustain this fragile
gift.

   At last, home looms near,
its familiar shape a soft
   benediction in gloom.

I carry my poem inside,
the roll unscathed yet
   changed by travel: like
me.

The walls do not care for
what I hold: they stand
mute, immune to the
tremors—

of creativity and
mortality. Yet, in this
quiet room, I find

space to unroll each
thought, to smooth out
    creases of worry, to
continue

the relentless quest of
creation, the fear and
   thrill of what might be
lost—

or what might, just
might, endure. Even as
   the world spins
indifferent, I

  scribe on, the act of
  writing a defiance, a
claim to existence:

    fragile, yet fierce. My
paper: a testament, a
    whispered challenge to
  the void.

Frostbound Musings

Cold seeps into bone: the
unyielding frost of dawn
mirrors my stiff words,

crystallized mid-flow. A
shard of breath hangs, a
   thought unfinished, a
  pause

too long and too cold.
Yet, outside, even now, a
few hardy birds sing.

   Their chirps slice
through the dense air:
defiance, or just
  survival? Unclear.

  My typewriter hesitates, like my
     breath on this sharp
morn, captured in
mid-air.

    The page blank, frosted,
a field after first snow,
impressions to make.

Mused by the chill,
thoughts like icebergs
float, much unseen, deep
beneath surface.

Each word I jot down a
footprint in new snow, a
   trail easily lost.

Nature's indifference
spreads wide around: the
sun's arc, cold yet
bright, aloof.

Insects crawl slowly,
resilient in the face of
frost's sharp dagger.

I envy their pace,
unrushed by the heat of
blood, or the burn of
time.

   The birds, undeterred,
flit with icy feathers,
quick, darting through
short days.

My thoughts freeze, then
thaw, a cycle tiresome,
like breath seen in cold
   air.

Inspiration flags, caught
in branches bare and
   slick, waiting for a
thaw.

This struggle with words:
is it merely Sisyphean, a
mountain never climbed?

Or is there pleasure,
hidden in the pushing,
  the weight we bear alone?

The rock rolls back down,
as do my unfinished
lines, drafts discarded,
cold.

Yet something stirs
still: the pleasure of
motion, of thoughts
taking shape, slow.

   These birds, those
insects; their mere
existence protests the
freeze they endure.

I, too, in my way,
pronounce a subtle
defiance: to write,
       though it's hard.

   The layers of ice build
up, not just outside, but
within, thick and numb.

   How I chip away, daily,
with typewriter as my pick,
words as faint warmth.

     Traffic hums outside, a
distant, muffled chorus,
life moving, ice-bound.

    Interruptions jar: the
     phone rings, a door slams
shut, piercing my ice
   cave.

Human patience thins,
like winter daylight,
fleeting, yet we push
onward.

It's in these moments,
cold clarity emerges:
create, despite frost.

Even Sisyphus might have
    admired the view, rock
perched at the peak.

And so with each word,
    each line pushing uphill,
I find my landscape's
edge.

Irony, bitter, frosts
over the sweetness of
task's completion, brief.

   The day's cold end comes,
and with it, a mix of
relief, tiredness, and
resolve.

Tomorrow, more frost,
more words, more uphill
battles: the poet's
winter.

These cycles of thought,
    repeated like seasons,
shift, show new paths in
snow.

Writing: a survival, a
resistance against the
encroaching blankness.

Words, my breath visible,
sculpted in air, linger,
then fade, but still
matter.

Each line a small heat,
against the day's deep
freeze, a spark held
   briefly aloft.

Commitment: a flame,
  flickering, persistent, a
light guiding through
   frost.

   My poem, my rock; heavy,
   yet mine to push, mine to
roll, mine to hold.

Through frozen mornings,
through the stasis of
  doubt, words spill, melt,
and reshape.

The commitment holds,
like ice on a bough,
waiting, poised for the
    thaw's touch.

Creativity, a puzzle of
ice crystals, unique,
   fragile, sharp.

The struggle, the strain,
yet also the clarity ice
   brings, the world honed.

A landscape revealed,
   stark and beautiful.

Tapestry of Contrasts

Love threads through the
weave of hate: we bind
    tightest where we tear,
and mend what's long been
broken: such is our
nature, cyclical, as the
moons wax and wane

    over this crowd gathered,
faces like pages: written
on, erased, rewritten:
scenes of love, brief as
blossoms, fierce as
storms, lasting in memory
alone:

but also hatred, woven
deep beneath the smiles,
the hellos, the embraces:
do we not cherish what
burns us, remember most
what hurt: the sting a
guide to the next step:

a play unfolds: actors in
ancient robes, voices
   raised in sorrow, chorus
lamenting: O fate, how
   you ensnare us, love and
hate in your net, taut
and unbreakable:

even in laughter, the
edge of something darker,
laughter that masks the
    growl of history,
       sweeping us along: who
has loved without the
shadow

of fear, the pulse of
loss: do we not dance on
the edge of a volcano,
waiting for the ground to
shift, for the fire
  beneath to claim its due?

yet, we toast, raise
glasses to what endures,
to the beauty crafted
from the ash, the art
that speaks of both loss
  and what's left to be
cherished:

politicians debate, a
spectacle of passion,
    theatrics masking or
revealing: do their words
aim to build, or to
uncover, to veil or lay
  bare conflicts?

and here, at the day's
    close, with the sun
      bleeding down the

horizon, all becomes a
jest, a line in a long
    dialogue with ourselves,
  with the world that
watches, mirth mingled
with resignation:

    no permanent harmony, no
final peace: just the
    move and countermove, the
    dance of opposites, the
rhythm: a chant, a spell
    against the silence that
will come, must come,

but not yet, not now: for
  now, let's revel in the
    fraught tapestry we
weave, every thread
pulled tight by our own
hands, every loop a
story, every knot a
    binding moment: so we
live, connected as we
are,

in love with what we
fear, hate what we
desire: a twist familiar
to any who've watched a
storm from the safety of
their windows, or kissed
with lips that tremble
from more than just cold.

This day ends, not with a
bang, but a chuckle, as
if the world knows the
joke's on us, and we know
it too, but play our
parts, hearts heavy or
   light, alone together in
     the vast, echoing stage.

So laugh, so cry, let
  your heart fill with the
music of now, the
dissonant chords that say
    this, too, is life, this
too is what it means to
be human: to hold, to
release, to meet again
  the ancient dance.

    210 embraces, 210
departures, each wave a
whisper of the sea's vast
conversation, each look a
   word in the dialogue of
  glance and gaze:
celebration and irony,
hand in hand, dancing.

Winter's Script

Sharp gusts sweep down:
narrow streets, whistle
   through wiry branches,
snatch away warmth: we
bundle closer, scarves
tight, faces half-buried.

These crowds, they
throng: a river of coats,
a flutter of bags, each
      face hidden: layers,
layers they carry their
   warmth like snails with
  shells.

Shadows stretch long:
elongation at noon,
distorted forms: they
dance, escape into the
shop fronts, melt with
the warmth inside.

We step in, the clamor:
products stack high,
shimmer like a winter
field's frost, but
   barren: no seeds here,
only the urge to possess.

Amid pines cut and
      stacked, I remember
      forests: each tree

spaced, a cosmos of its
own, roots interlinked,
silent.

Here, the music loops, a
tinny echo of joy, devoid
of spirit, a tune
repeated until it grates,
like an old clock's
　monotonous chime.

We age, our worlds
contract: boundaries
　drawn tighter, paths
well-trodden, the
unknowns sifted out,
comfort in the familiar.

Every face looks the
same, blur of winter
hats, swift steps, the
　　eyes do not meet: we turn
inward, the mind's
landscape now a circle,
not expansive.

We buy little,
necessities, a nod to the
ritual: gift-giving,
　though it feels more like
　　giving in, a concession
to the expanse we once
traversed eagerly.

Leaving, the cold bites
    again, its teeth sharp:
each breath a reminder of
the narrowing pathways:
    blood vessels constrict,
a metaphor: life's
closing circle.

The drive back, heater
    on, the road's familiar
  turns, each bend a
repetition, each mile a
mantra: home, home, home.

In our garden, the bare
twigs: each a script, a
calligraphy of survival:
they hold the winter's
weight, a promise of
spring, of renewal.

But tonight, the sky
looms, endless: a fabric
stretched taut by cold
    hands, stars pierce the
      dark: sharp, like
memories, distant but
      present.

We make tea, the kettle's
    purr a comforting rumble,
domestic rituals: they
    tether, each act a
thread, woven into the
fabric of days.

The shrinking, perhaps
not a loss, but a
distillation: essences
emerge, purer, the
clutter falls away,
   leaving only the vital.

At the window, I watch:
the night deepens, frost
  whispers to the glass, a
   conversation: cold,
insistent, I listen,
learning still.

Life's lessons, like
frost, form in the cold,
   clarity arrived at, not
    despite, but because of
the narrowing, each cold,
    each isolation a teacher.

  We ready for bed, the
room's soft contours
familiar, safe: our world
   smaller, yes, but each
part beloved, known,
touched with care.

  Sleep comes, a closing:
not just of eyes, but of
    hands, holding tight what
matters, the day's cold a
memory, the warmth here,
between us.

Tomorrow, the sun will
rise, cold and clear: it
    will not warm much, but
    it will light up what's
important, and we, in our
small world, will see it
well.

Solstice Shadows

The day leans short:
slight, the dimming sun
folds early, curls
beneath the horizon's
    blanket: shadows stretch,
      a tender gloom.

Yet: there is light in
the scant hours, crisp
    and deliberate, sharp as
    the breath that fogs
  before my face.

In the stillness, each
    leafless branch balances
  a history: ancient,
gnarled scripts, telling
of survival.

I ponder, pacing along
the frozen path: each
  moment's weight is the
weight of light, fleeting
yet full.

A bird, quick against the
   slow splay of dusk, jets
    – an ink spot on the
sky's pale page:
contrasts script the day.

    Does it know of
solstices, or does it
meet the chill
    unquestioning,
unwavering?

I string lights on the
    tree: small beacons,
    pulsing bright, a dotted
line guiding: come here,
warmth waits.

Each bulb a miniature
sun, tucked in pine's
sharp arms, holding off
the immense night: each a
defiance, a point of
persistence.

A laugh escapes me,
    shaking a limb: a
    snowfall from pine
needles, winter's
confetti: brief,
celebratory.

    This shortest day: a
    breath held, then
released into longer
    tomorrows, the promise
    whispering.

How quickly a year slips
    – granular, like sand,
through the tightened
   waist of an hourglass.

   The tree, labelled "Grown
in Canada," stands
adorned in my living
room, a migrant from
   colder soils: has it,
too, felt the tug of
  changing latitudes, the
shift from seed to
sentinel?

Below its boughs, gifts
wrapped in glossy reds
and silvers, hug the
contours of anticipation:
what joy to give, to
receive, to be encircled.

   Here, in the quiet, with
the ticking clock
      celebrating each second
   known to darkness, I find
solace in rhythm: the
   predictable heart of the
home.

As twilight consolidates,
I pour tea, steam rising
like spirits into softer
shadows: I sip, the

warmth spreading, echoing
the distant sun.

Outside, the world holds
   its breath, crystalline
in its waiting,
frost-limned and perfect:
   a static pause between
the inhale of galaxies,
   the exhale of dusk.

Yet, even paused, the
microcosms bustle:
   crystals forming, icicles
lengthening by minute
contributions, nature's
artisans at work.

The cycle continues,
   unhindered by our notions
of stop, of end, of
darkness too deep: life
whispers even in the
coldest reach.

Birds settle on bare
branches, their bodies
small orbs of life:
resilient, resistant to
the pull of winter's
   sleepy charm.

How delicate their dance,
aloft from the starkness
   of stripped bark: flit
and flutter, a punctuated
   rhythm in the silent air.

   And tomorrow, the shift
subtle: minutes stitched
to the edge of darkness,
a hem letting out light,
gradual, gracious.

  I, too, move in small
     increments, a creature of
  cycles: breathing in the
   year's tight close,
  breathing out renewal.

Each solstice marks, not
   just the sun's sway, but
the pivot of souls, a
calibration of hearts
towards what is tiny,
tender, against the vast
     cold.

The tree glimmers, each
light a soft explosion of
  triumph: here, brightness
resides, here, in the
  confluence of shadow and
glow, I stand, rooted,
yet reaching.

Temporal Whispers

Leaf after leaf: the
voyage of autumn's slow
decay, each shedding a
   whisper: time is the
     brush, we are the
   painting, fleeting though
   touched by forever. Paths
we roamed, the dog and I:
his paws were soft
chronicles, padded with
the dust of our days,
  every grain, every stir:
    memories we cannot
reclaim. He ran ahead, as
if chasing the hours,
  down the windy orchard,
  his form blurred against
the rush of the world,
heart pulsing with the
thrill of the chase:
alive and ignorant of
conclusion.

The sudden stillness the
   day he fell: how small a
frame becomes when life
   departs. The ground, hard
and cold, refused our
pleas, nature's
indifferent gaze folding
back upon itself.

I learned then: control
is an illusion, thin as
   the membrane between now
and then, between breath
and silence. The universe
     whispers in a syntax of
loss: everything
connects, detaches.

Atoms, those tiny
persistences, hold
together, then don't: our
composition is temporary,
our bonds, momentary. A
     dog's warmth, a boy's
laugh, diffusing into
     autumn air.

His fur, once vibrant,
     faded into the landscape,
reclaimed by the very
earth it once eagerly
   explored. What cycles
through must cycle back:
energy borrowed must be
returned.

I remember the weight of
him, heavy not in mass
but in absence, the
density of emptiness
shaping the contours of
   my arms. Every step I
take stirs echoes, paw

    prints on the soft earth
    of memory: each
indentation a mark of
what was and what can
never be again.

Through it all, the sky
watches, vast and
unchanging: keeper of
every fleeting thing,
silent witness to every
loss, every resurrection.
It knew his name, and it
knows mine, threading us
together in the thin
    fabric of its blue
expanse.

Years peel off, like bark
from a seasoned trunk,
each layer uncovering not
youth, but clarity: the
sharpness of finite days.
We orbit around our
griefs, planets held in
    the gravity of what we
cannot hold.

Time: it heals because it
erodes, wearing away the
sharp edges of our
sorrows, softening them
    into the manageable
    texture of narrative. He

exists now in stories,
paw steps in the hallway
of thought, his bark a
   note in the symphony of
the past.

   Change is not an event,
but a process: it unfolds
as a flower does, petal
by petal falling open,
 revealing the heart of
things: all that lives
must perish, and all that
dies has once lived
fiercely.

We share this thread,
stretching across the
 infinite cloth of
existence: the dog, the
boy, now the man: all
phases of the same
   matter, reshaped but
constant, a continuum of
essence.

I think of him, not as
gone, but as transformed:
   elements dispersed, but
spirit intact, his
   presence a subtle
gravity, a gentle warping
   of my orbit.

So, I walk on, steps
measured by the thrum of
   a universe in constant
   motion: every atom a
testament to the tales of
transformation. The heart
keeps its own time, its
beat a testament to all
we've loved and lost, its
   rhythm the echo of paws,
of footsteps, of
heartbeats fused, then
     unfused. This, the fabric
  of our lives, woven with
   threads of joy and the
inevitable snags of pain.

   And in the end, we are all
passing landscapes,
   fleeting imprints,
shadows cast by a turning world.
   We linger only as long
  as memory holds us, as long
as love recalls our shape.

   The dog, the boy, the man—
each phase dissolves
 into the next,
 not lost, but carried forward,
folded into the breath of wind,
   the hush of leaves, the hush
of time itself.

Nothing vanishes—
    it only shifts, reshapes,
  whispers on.

Contrast in Spoonfuls

    A craving stirred in
sleep: soft, sweet desire
for a taste of ice cream,
    vanilla, perhaps, or a
swirl of something rich
    and dark with chocolate:
night indulges whims.

The cold creaminess
seemed an innocent wish,
a simple joy, under
moon's patient eye. Yet,
as morning rose, petals
of light unfurling,

  the radio crackles and
life pitches: a ship, it
  reports, flames engulfing
  its skeleton at sea:
sirens, smoke, the terror
of heat.

How does such a day begin
with thoughts so trivial
as the choice between
scoops or cones –

  only to collide with
despair so vast it
swallows horizons, drowns
all sweeter thoughts in
its dark, salted depths?

The disconnect is brutal:
cream turns to ash in the
mind's tentative grasp of
 a world where pleasure
  and catastrophe are
   neighbors in time.

Ripples of news spread,
 circling out: families,
futures lost to
unforgiving flame. What
design can there be in
such randomness where joy
 and horror lie side by
side?

Each bite now feels like
an affront to those
fighting for breath,
 beneath unforgiving
waves, their cries a
stark music against my
mundane tongue tasting
sweetness.

The sweetness burns,
contrasts so sharp they
 tear at the fabric of
understanding. Here, a
simple craving, there, a
complex tragedy: life's
textures differ, bluntly
juxtaposed.

Is there a lesson in this
juxtaposition, or merely
the chaos of existence,
patterns ascribed to
unfathomable randomness,
threads we weave to keep
    from unraveling?

   The ice cream melts,
     unused, a pool of
   potential joy gone tepid,
reflecting the smoky
silhouettes of an inferno
at sea, where heat
consumes more than just
fuel.

Such is the morning's
harsh lesson: the taste
of loss mingling with the
ice cream's sweet
dissolve, both sharing
    the same brief moment in
a spoon.

Across these moments,
life's vast spectrum
spreads: laughter, death,
the cry of gulls
overhead, indifferent, or
  maybe just attuned to
  cycles we're too enmeshed
  within to grasp.

In this, perhaps, there
lies a whisper of the
divine, or merely the
    echoes of our own limited
sight, bound by the
  horizon we know, ignoring
    the broader sky.

This contrast, so natural
    yet so violently imposed,
    questions the order we
impose on chaos, the
narratives built to keep
the void at bay, simple
  pleasures a veneer over
    the abyss.

With each lick, the world
  shifts, slightly, as if
to remind me: what is,
simply is, and living is
the delicate balance
between embracing the now
and mourning the
inevitable.

Thus the day unfolds:
between spoons and smoke,
between the embrace of
mundane delights and the
    inescapable tragic that
    awaits: a cycle, a
pendulum swinging,
unceasing, from trivial
  to transcendent.

And so I sit, spoon
paused, ice cream
dripping, listening to
   the crackle of despair
   miles away, fire meeting
water, all while sun
   dares to shine still on
such an odd, mixed-up
world.

   Can we ever make sense of
      life's layered song, its
melding of minor and
major keys?

Cyclic Bonds

Gathered closely by the
fire, our voices mingle
and lift: a delicate,
rising choir that shivers
    like smoke, adrift.

Outside, the cold
sharpens, steeling the
    night's black edge,
    divisions harden:
nature's relentless
wedge.

Hearts thaw in shared
light, melting frost with
warm tales, but shadows
grow with the night, as
    every union entails.

We are fragments seeking
wholeness, yet splinting
further apart: this the
  dance, timeless, played
on a human heart.

Under the same immense
sky, our stories
intertwine, like branches
    aiming high only to
        individually define.

Each leaf whispers
lineage, stirred by the
winter gust, speaking in
　its own language: in
　　unity, in distrust.

The pulse of connection
beats, rising and
　　falling: a tide that, by
its very feats, forged
channels where we divide.

We reach across the
　chasms, hands clasped,
eyes locked, in fleeting
panoramas, before doors
are knocked

by the winds of change,
or the quakes of fate:
alliances rearrange, and
　　love dissolves in hate.

　Doesn't every season
declare the impermanence
of bond? Trees bare, laid
　　stark and bare, roots
　deep, far beyond.

The cycle of gathering,
　then dispersing like
seeds, is nature's own
　harboring of our deepest
　needs.

Conflicts, small but sharp, cut through the veneer of peace, revealing, beneath the tarp, the age-old human lease

on temporary truces, on love that must expire: time introduces entropy's quiet choir.

And so we drift, again,
   like continents in slow
     part: our era's refrain
etched deep in the heart.

In every handshake
  lingered or in words left
unsaid, unity is
  fingered, then slips
     through like thread.

  We, ever in motion, like Earth's molten core, hold love like an ocean that touches each shore.

Yet divisions are tectonic, shifting silent, deep: the world's ironic promise that we
  keep.

And though we aim for
steadiness, for a land
without divide, in our
  grasp is readiness for
the spreading tide.

Christmas brings a
starlit peace, a brief,
  shimmering truce, where
conflicts seem to cease,
    and goodwill gets its
use.

But even stars flicker
out, and carols fade
  away, leaving room for
doubt, and night after
the day.

Aging, like a narrowing
    path, guides us through
chilled air, each step a
quiet math calculating
care.

In the end, these
    gatherings, these
fractures, these
renewals, are but
    markings, ephemeral
jewels.

The light dims, guests
take leave, the night
reclaims its due, and I,
both grieve and renew.

Nature cycles, unfazed by
our human comings,
goings, eternal sky
    forever showing

that from unity to
division, from gathering
to alone, is but a vision
    of the cycle known.

Thus resigned, yet
hopeful still, in the
  dance of ebb and flow,
find the will to let go,

    acknowledge this: our
    plight, our shared,
    cyclic breath, holding
tight unto death.

  Yet in this revolving
  door, a truth quietly
spoken: to love, to
explore, even when
broken.

So let the cycle turn,
let divisions come and
 fade, for in them, we
learn how togetherness is
 made.

Internal Fireworks

The cold slips under the
door: silence into
    silence, yet inside, a
  carnival kicks up, a
whirring, sparking show.

My thoughts crackle
    without pause: roman
      candles, each idea its
own vibrant star,
bursting too bright to
hold.

The window shows a still
life: frost etching its
slow art, trees stand,
muted and precise, their
calm, a sharp contrast.

I pace a pattern in the
    rug, trying to align my
    steps with slower,
quieter rhythms: it's a
dance I can't master.

    Beneath, electrons whirl,
neurons firing in festive
revolt, a loud parade on
    a quiet street, like
    someone forgot to tell
them.

To simmer down, to
breathe deep, a directive
   lost in the flurry, the
fizzle and pop of
   synaptic jets, each a
   flare, lighting up.

The world may rest in
ice, but I am ablaze: a
fire set not to warm but
to wonder, each spark a
question, burning.

   I try to cup them,
contain or command this
   fierce energy, but it's
   like seizing sunbeams, a
futile, foolish grab at
light.

The day drifts, time
   freezing and thawing in
   erratic ticks, while I'm
swept in vibrant
torrents, a river that
   knows no banks.

Outside, a cardinal
flits, red blip against
the grey tableau, a shock
of life in dormant scene,
mirroring my relentless
surge.

I envy the ice its slow
creep, the snow's quiet
layering, each flake a
whisper, settling: how I
    long for such a hush.

But here, inside, the
    festival roars on,
uninvited but insistent,
    and I, host to this
rebellion, find no peace
in the clamor.

Sometimes, thought is an
ember that refuses to
die, but glows
dangerously, as if to
  remind: control is
illusion, embrace the
burn.

  By evening, the fireworks
do not tire, but I,
spectator, find a strange
solace in the display, my
own private wildness
known.

To laugh at the chaos,
    maybe, to find humor in
the explosive mind, where
calm should be but isn't:
a joke shared with
myself.

The marvel is not in the
  quiet external, but in
the riotous internal, the
unceasing show of
  thought, relentless,
beautiful.

As night deepens, the
external world freezes
more firmly, its
  stillness a stark canvas,
my mind the relentless
painter.

  I accept this, the
internal chaos, as part
of the landscape, no
longer a disruption but a
    pulse I recognize, vital.

This is the rhythm of my
being, erratic beats,
  unexpected bursts, a
  symphony of synapses,
firing: the music of a
mind alive.

  The fireworks continue,
unabated, a celebration
of existence, each spark
  a fleeting brilliance,
dying only to light
again.

With this, I find my
peace, not in silence,
but in accepting the
noise, the vivid chaos,
as the heartbeat of my
   thoughts.

   The day closes, the
internal show still
     vibrant as ever: I drift
   to sleep amidst the
  fireworks, restless, yet
strangely complete.

Shadow's Whisper

    Winter light bends: soft
gray films over the sharp
edges of noon: this
    season's breath is cold
   and slow, guiding my
thoughts into shadows
that stretch, shrink,
like a mind changing.

The flicker of a branch's
shadow: quick as a
  murmuration's shift, or
slow as the pull of dark
tides beneath silver
moonlight: all is
movement, all is flux
even when seeming still.

   A leaf, crisp and curled,
skitters across
frost-hardened soil: is
 it driven by wind, or by
the subtle carving paths
of decay and life? Thus,
each element connects,
  tethered by invisible
strings.

  What does this dimming
   tell? Is there truth in
     the closing day or merely
   the illusion crafted by

    the angle of sunset,
slicing through bare
   trees, casting long
fingers that probe the
limits of sight and
   sense?

Light, in its dying
flares, brushes the
surfaces: walls, the
silent watchful windows,
a lone cat padded across
the sill, unhurried: its
  eyes catching the last
dull gleams, mirrors to
    the fading day.

   Particles, hanging in the
air, make a stage of
beams, each mote
performing in this quiet
theatre of the afternoon:
do they dance for their
own joy, or for the eyes
that catch their brief
brilliance?

Here, in this transition,
I stand, watching the
deepening of the
afternoon, each minute a
    soft click in the watch
   of the year, each second
a smoothing of the sharp

   angles of reality,
blurred serenely.

The cold bites gently, a
reminder of time passing,
   of seasons cycling in
their endless loop: from
   birth to death, from
light to darkness, back
again: how small, this
  human frame in the vast
choreography of cosmos.

Shadows deepen into
shapes, figments or
realities— hard to say: a
bush might be a
slumbering beast; a tree,
a waiting sage; stones
  could whisper of ancient
days if only we knew how
to hear them beneath
their frosted silence.

Perception itself seems a
   shadow, uncertain,
wavering with the light's
whim: what is seen is not
always what is, and what
is might not show its
face easily, hidden
beneath folds of light.

A dog barks, cracking the
scene: sound waves ripple
through the cold, clear
air, breaking the spell
of visual trance: life
stirs, refuses to be
merely a spectator of
   light's play, insists on
      its own voice.

   Night approaches, a deep
      blue stain spreading
across the canvas of day:
   does darkness reveal or
does it conceal? I ponder
this, wrapped in my coat,
the chill urging a
   retreat to warmth.

Yet, in this moment of
   retreat, curiosity
     blooms, defiant against
     the encroaching gloom:
what lies within these
shifts, these soft
gradations from light to
dark? What lessons are
written in the interplay
of visible and hidden?

The world turns,
inevitably: the winter's
   night seals the day's
conversation, leaving

questions hanging like
stars, unreachable yet
  illuminative: I carry
them, small lights
    flickering within, as I
  move toward warmth
inside.

Tomorrow, again, the
light will shift, change,
    cast new shadows, offer
new angles: and I,
perhaps wiser, perhaps
    not, will continue to
watch, to learn the
    language of light, its
soft syllables, its harsh
strokes, its endless,
silent poetry.

Predatory Melodies

    beyond the glass: a cold
that seeps, a world that
feeds on itself:
predation is the stark
  melody played on leaf,
branch, and under soil:
where worms turn in the
    dark, escaping the early
bird's quest for morning
sustenance,

the frost outlines each
blade of grass— a razor
edge to the day that cuts
as it nourishes, life as
predation, a concept as
harsh as it is true; the
robin plunges, comes up
with its reward, a
  wriggling testament to
survival's demand,

sipping coffee, warmth
spreads in concentric
circles from cup to
  heart, comfort juxtaposed
with the raw hunt going
    forth outside my window,
    where survival is no
philosophical thought,
but a visceral need

fed through the simple
   act of engulfing, of
   energies transferred, one
body to another, with no
   mind for mercy, no pause
for the moral queries
that bind a human heart:
predators, clad in fur,
scales, feathers, execute
nature's dark commands
without a second's doubt,

observing these dynamics,
from my insulated view, I
   unravel the threads of
food chains: complex,
interwoven systems that
do not falter, do not
   forgive, each creature
   embedded deeply in this
   wheel of consumption,
  from the wolf to the
lamb, from the hawk to
the field mouse, each
life another's aliment,
fated

to fuel the ceaseless
   engine of existence, and
here, safe in heated
comfort, the reality
  stark: I am no different,
part of this vast
      organism of Earth where
   we feed, and are fed

upon, our moral
complexities dissolved
when viewed through the
lens of biology, wherein
every action is about
　survival,

just as plants reach for
the sun, just as fungi
break down the dead, we
partake in the cycle,
　　　unknowingly or with full
　　　awareness, as when we
　　prepare our daily
sustenance, from sources
that once breathe, moved,
lived as fervently as the
predator pursues its
prey; a meal is a quiet
echo of the chase,

witnessed in the fog, as
light fails, and in that
failing light, nature
does not pause but shifts
　its tactics, the night
bringing a new set of
hunters into the dark
playground, their eyes
　　　adapted to the minimal
　　glow, their senses honed
　　　for nocturnal raids, the
owl's silent swoop, the
　　　fox's low creep,

as the day completes its
   cycle, I turn back
indoors, to artificial
lights and the hum of a
refrigerator, a modern
cave's comforts, yet
outside, the relentless
logic of eat or be eaten
  continues to spin its
    ancient and endless
thread, weaving through
each action, sleep, or
  wake, and I, no more than
a node in this network,
  savor the solace of my
warm abode,

    accepting, with a sigh,
the reality that binds
   every living thing: this
   planet pulses not just
  with life but with the
omnipresent demand of
death, a demand that
   feeds the living,
ensuring that tomorrow,
  predators will wake,
hungry again, ready to
partake in the eternal
  ritual, as old as life
itself.

Temporal Continuance

Moments fall: each second
  a tiny infinity, caught
in the swift: turn of
years—

We stand at the height:
of December's tail,
balancing: on the thin
line, uttering farewells
to numbers that fade,
like stars at dawn.

The night air: thick with
    promises, laughter rolls
in waves: across the
    cold: tick of the clock.

Outside, the sky is a
play of lights, children
believe in the magic: of
new starts, eyes dazzle
with flashes, sparkling
reflections.

Yet, here I am: musing
  over the rinse and
    repetition, wondering: if
the champagne fizz is
just another loop, in the
    grand: cycle of cosmos.

Change is but an
agreement: we make with
time, to feel like
   architects of our own
   destinies, marking a day
as rebirth: while seasons
heed no man's pause.

People chant numerical
downfalls: five, four,
   three, embracing: in the
   confetti drift, clusters
  of hope knit in the air:
as if time wears
  renewals.

What's so new: in the
    stroke of midnight? Does
  the universe: even sigh,
    or does it too smirk, at
  our tiny celebrations,
   while spiraling:
endlessly in its
vastness?

Yet the charm: of
illusion: compels us— to
    dress up, sing out, to
   link arms underneath: the
   cold glow of stars,
believing in the beat: of
collective hearts.

I hear the ecstasies: of
neighbors, the boom and
crackle that slice: the
somber silence of my
room: where I sit,
pondering the cyclic:
dance of atoms.

And I laugh, not with
cynicism but with a
tender: amusement, at our
splendid folly, our human
condition: to see the
flip of a calendar: as a
giant leap.

We tick: toward the
inevitable, the grand
continuance, the same sun
rising, not a fresh sun,
not a fresh light: but a
familiar warmth: greeting
us, like an old friend.

So the fireworks explode—
a symphony: for the
cosmos, ignored by the
cosmos, yet cherished: in
human hearts, a
spectacle: of sparks,
soon to fade into the
night's deep canvas.

One year melds into:
another, the sequence:
unbroken, as we spin:
joyously, woefully, in
    the arms: of the same old
    galaxy, dressed briefly:
in new numbers.

Temporal Threshold

Winter's cold hand: it
touches each silent, bare
branch, where birdsong
　once lived: a muted
symphony.

　The year turns, a page:
　　softly, almost unheard
underneath the bustle and
bright bursts of
fireworks.

Here I stand: at the edge
of the old and the new,
　pondering time's fabric—
woven, unraveling.

Is it a mere seam we
cross, or a profound
shift in depths unseen?
　The stars are
　indifferent: their
　glimmer, ageless.

　　I listen to the silence:
it speaks of the hours
spent, the moments lost:
how many breaths?

The New Year sighs
gently: a child, unaware
of its burdens, its
gifts. What will it know?
What will it forget?

Continuity: a myth we
tend like a hearth fire.
Yet, change whispers
through cracks, a draft
    unsettling the warm air.

I think of resolutions:
frail vessels on time's
  vast ocean, carried
forward, swallowed whole,
or reshaped by relentless
tides.

   The cycle: a promise or a
     pretense? Each January
    resembles the last.
Still, we mark it, a
notch on nature's ancient
doorframe.

Outside, the world
celebrates: loud, eager,
   vibrant. Inside, I
  embrace the quiet revelry
  of thought, of being.

Past and future: two ends
of the same thread I
hold, tight and slack in
turns, wondering where it
leads.

A leaf, caught in a
　winter gust, twirls: a
simple dance against
　complex skies. Does it
know its path? Do I?

Each second ticks:
unique, irreplaceable.
Yet, form a chain linking
everything and nothing,
　all at once.

As fireworks paint the
night, I see time's face:
　old as eternity, new as
the spark that fades
before it's fully seen.

Questions linger, float
　like the smoke after the
light: what changes with
the shift of calendars?
What remains?

　The cosmos spins: silent,
　indifferent to human
declarations. Yet, we

claim this moment, dress
it in significance.

    My own heart beats a
quiet drum: not
celebration, nor
resignation, but a rhythm
    of continued search.

    The threshold underfoot,
firm yet imaginary— do I
step over, or simply
acknowledge its presence?

The New Year: it
   breathes, slow, like a
creature at rest. Does it
   dream? Of what—a
   beginning, an end?

Voices rise in the
distance: joyful,
  hopeful. Here, I balance
between epochs, feeling
both detached and
integral.

    Observing the old year's
retreat, its lessons
   etched deep: the joys
   shared, the griefs
weathered, the mundane
and the profound.

Forward, the uncharted
stretches: mysteries
cloaked in the ordinary.
Will this turning bring
 revelation or repetition?

Every atom in me, every
leaf, every star—
connected in the silent
 dance of existence, of
endurance.

As the countdown echoes,
a part of me joins in,
tentative. Another part
stands back: an observer.

 Midnight strikes: a chime
that resonates in the
marrow. Time moves, or we
move through it—
philosophical, yet
 visceral.

And so the night unfolds,
the new year stepping
 lightly across the
threshold of my thoughts,
 a guest uninvited,
inevitable.

Fireworks dwindle, a last
   spark in the darkness.
New year, like every
   other: familiar, yet
   unexplored.

  As the revelers sleep,
dreams mingling with
reality, I remain awake:
watching, waiting,
wondering.

  Simple questions,
profound as stars: what
is changed? What is the
same? In this annual
   rebirth, what truly is
reborn?

The cold sharpens, a
reminder of continuity:
seasons circle in their
ancient dance.

Indifferent Light

   Cold light slices through
the frosted window: like
arrows, yet blunt, my
lungs catch each breath:
harsh, unwanted clarity
mixed with the typical
gray of winter thoughts.

   The body: a vessel feebly
crafted, prone to stagger
  under invisible weights,
 a clear sky mocks my
congested chest: nature
unfolds unheeded by human
   frailty.

Crystals form on the
sill: a universe frozen,
expanding minutely in
fractal patterns: wonders
small enough to go
  unnoticed, unless one is
   forced, as I am, to
stillness, to observation
 broken by coughs.

Sunlight holds a promise:
  fresh, relentless,
insistent as the seasons'
shifting gears: yet I
    remain the same, rooted
   in the old year's
lingering shadow.

What divides today from
yesterday? Arbitrary
lines: as the calendar
turns, so do our
expectations, but the
   cold has no calendar,
     ignores our neat
separations of time and
  duty.

Layers of warmth, bundled
ineffectively: I face the
  chill that pierces
  synthetic fibers, nudging
closer to bone, as if to
remind me: all constructs
are porous, the cold, an
unwelcome truth
infiltrator of flesh.

The sun climbs:
   indifferent, a stark
white disk in a pale blue
    vault: and I wonder, do
its photons feel the
futility of warming a
body so locked in battle
with itself?

   Day stretches out like a
path untaken, edges
blurred by the bright
   gleam that deceives the
eye, promising more than

it delivers: much like my
  intentions, bright at the
onset, dulled by the
  reality of my limits.

In this silence, where
one hears the settling
house, the distant bark,
   the muted shuffle of
neighborly feet: I am
adrift in my own
enclosure, my breath
visible, a sign of life
in the still air.

To desire engagement, to
live fully in the moment:
easy in theory, an
Everest in practice,
especially when each
movement is a labor, each
thought burdened with the
weight of tired flesh.

  And yet, there is a kind
of peace in surrender, in
admitting not all battles
   are to be fought, not all
      days seized. Today the
mind must wander alone,
unaccompanied by the
body's enthusiastic
sprint.

The sun's arc declines,
unnoticed by many but not
 by me: I've watched it
trace its indifferent
course across the sky,
its light a cold comfort

 to the bones I carry
wearily, promising
nothing but the passing
 of time, the slow shift
from one form to another:
from solid to shadow,
 from pain to acceptance.

As dusk approaches, the
clarity of morning
becomes memory, frost
 retreating in the face of
night's soft
 encroachment. My thoughts
turn toward sleep, toward
the hope of a body
restored by rest, by the
 quiet hum of a world
slowing down, drawing
 breath.

Here, in the closing of
 day, I find a quiet
acceptance: change,
 whether of self or
season, comes not with
fanfare but the slow tick

    of the clock, patient,
persistent, unyielding to
desire or despair.

And so another year
begins, not with steps
but glances: backward at
the path worn, forward
into the
    uncertain light: where
time's indifferent hands
    shape both memory and
hope into a single
    breath, held briefly,
then released into the
    vast and patient dark.

Temporal Dichotomy

The morning breaks:
heavy, the air thick with
a silence, my body, a
leaden vessel, still, yet
   thoughts spin: restless
   weavers at looms that
never pause: how they
     dart, silver fish in a
  dark stream.

  My fevered forehead, a
touchstone to measure the
day's unyielding heat:
     body sunk deep in the
    mattress's grasp, mind
afloat, untethered,
    soaring high above this
temporal cage.

Why does the flesh fail
  while the spirit insists
to dance, wildly, amid
pulsars and nebulae—and
  the quiet room holds a
    man captive, bound in
blankets: his universe.

   Contrast this: the
vibrant neuron-space,
vast and electric,
against the slow, painful
inch of movement, limb by

 limb, breath by breath:
irony of a divided
existence.

Cells divide, renew, the
body's quiet labor,
 unnoticed until
delayed—then every task
becomes a titan's
challenge, the simplest
 act a mythic ordeal.

Yet, there: the mind
wanders, a discoverer,
 through thoughts light
 and crisp as autumn
leaves that scatter ahead
 of footsteps still not
taken, paths not tread.

A pen lies beside the
 notebook, idle: it mocks
 with potential, a river
of ink stilled by the dam
 of aching sinews— and the
words that bubble up are
caught, choked back down
 by a throat tight with
the day's discomfort.

An unfair race, this:
energy unseen doesn't
tire, doesn't fade, while
muscle, bone, skin—my

earthy components— demand
   respite, whisper of
limits that the mind
tends to forget or,
perhaps, refuses to
   acknowledge.

Outside, the world turns
indifferently to my
 plight: birds swoop,
chirping their morning
hymns to vitality; trees
sway, resilient in their
rooted strength; even the
sun pulls itself higher,
   undaunted by the small
dramas ensconced within
walls.

 This room, a chamber of
stillness, holds a
solitary figure: man of
clay and spirit, at war
   within himself, where
     malaise lays a heavy, wet
blanket over all intents
and ambitions.

 Each breath, a labor: the
lungs fill, the chest
 rises, painfully slow,
then a release that never
quite frees: this cycle,
a microcosm of trying and

failing, then trying once
   more.

How cruel, this split:
the agility of thought,
unbounded, versus the
confined rebellion of a
corpus unwilling or
unable to follow suit, to
   chase the flight of
ideas: skyward, swift.

As day leans into its
   afternoon arc, the
contrast sharpens: mind
racing along the bright
edges of dreams and
schemes, while the body
lies fallow, a field
after harvest: depleted.

What lessons to draw from
this dissonance, this
   jarring duet of capacity
and incapacity? Is there
wisdom in the
   frustration, a purpose in
   the forced pause, a
   message scripted in the
language of limitation?

   The day wanes; shadows
stretch, thin and long,
   across the floor,

reaching toward a bed
where stillness is both
   prison and refuge, and a
man contemplates the
unfairness of a race run
   on two different tracks:
one of flesh, the other
of thought.

And so, with night's
approach, the balance
shifts slightly, a
reluctant truce between
   the cerebral and the
corporeal: each
   acknowledges the other,
   their intertwined fate, a
shared journey through
   the hours, bound by the
same temporal thread.

Yet as sleep's embrace
   draws near, it is not
surrender but rather a
   quiet acknowledgment:
that mind and flesh must
   meet somewhere between
flight and falling, must
   find in limitation's
cradle a different kind
   of freedom, where rest
becomes not defeat but
   transformation, where
dreams bridge the gap
   between what soars and

what lies still, until
   dawn parts them once
again.

Transmutation Harmonies

Old tunes, dust-laden: I
   carried them, their
cracked cases like
   brittle leaves, to the
store's bright lights and
cooler air: a refresh, a
cleansing of sorts.

Scanning shelves, my
   fingers trace the spines
   of now and then: Bach
here replaces Byrd, a
shift in chords and
perhaps in heart.

Every plucked string that
vibrates in the air is
   more than mere music;
it's the thrum of time
changing, the pulse of
   old worlds receding.

How fluidly the new fills
gaps left by the outworn,
   a tide washing over the
   sand's imprinted past—
it's not loss, this
giving over, but
   transformation.

The clerk nods as I hand
   over my relic tunes; his
   smile a bridge spanning
decades compressed into
musical scores.

   Behind me, racks of vinyl
whisper secrets of
revolution and quiet
evolutions: somehow, the
beat of a drum machine
feels like progress.

In the corner, a
turntable spins, needle
dropped on a track that
will soon become my
     latest haunt, my new
tradition in old ritual's
clothing.

I stand amidst echoes and
       emerging melodies,
   feeling myself woven into
the loom of rhythms that
beat out the old, usher
in the new.

The record spins, and
with each revolution, it
   seems my spirit lifts a
   bit from its deep ruts,
   the familiar paths carved
by years of play.

Johann's structured
  harmonies lend order to
my thoughts, unscrambling
chaos as neatly as
    dividing lines in a
stanza, each note a
measured step.

  Leaving the old songs
felt like pruning dead
branches, making room for
  fresh growth, for green
shoots that will one day
flower into sound.

  Bach is different, not
    just in melody or time,
    but in essence: his music
swirls like autumn winds,
    catching up leaves once
settled, now adrift.

And isn't that the way of
things? Hold too tightly
      and you're just clutching
at air, at notes that
  have long since faded
into the quiet.

    This is renewal, not
simply exchange of one
good for another, but a
deeper alchemy,
transmuting worn grooves
into paths yet trodden.

   So I sit, newly purchased
vinyl underarm, and feel
an alignment, a tuning to
frequencies that pulse
  with the now, resonating
with the core of change.

Each song that plays is
   both a farewell and a
greeting: to past loves,
to former selves, to all
  the echoes we leave
behind in the grooves.

And in the music, I find
not just notes, but
   spaces between, where
  possibilities hang,
suspended, waiting for
the play.

The record store fades as
  I step into the cool
evening, the air itself
seems to hum with a
newfound clarity, a
crispness that wasn't
there before.

   Home, the turntable
waits, its arm poised to
begin its dance across
  the landscape of bumps
and dips that tell of
Bach's deep thought.

And as the first notes
    spill into the room, I
understand: this is more
than music; it's a map to
uncharted lands within
me.

  So let the old records
    rest, let them gather
dust in someone else's
  corner: I have found a
new groove, etched with
the promise of now.

Listening, the world
realigns, each note a
  polestar, guiding my
wandering thoughts to
harbors new,
    where Bach's mathematics
of sound transform the
    familiar into fresh
wonder: each measure a
  doorway through which
yesterday's music
    becomes tomorrow's
revelation, the vinyl's
  spiral groove an endless
path to grace.

Sunlight on Feathers

   The jay: small vigor,
    life concentrated: beams
catch: sunlight in its
   feathers:

   Fluff: expansion: warmth:
each barb releasing
light, particles dance,
    gleam:

So simple, this sun bath,
yet profound in its
   ritual, instinct: layered
     deep:

Feeding on the solar, it
shivers, shifts, splendid
against vast blue:

   Not merely survival— this
  is joy, small and pure, a
display, unnoticed:

Look closer: complexity
in the fluffing, precise
as a clock's tick:

Feathers, splayed: a
mesh, catching rays,
  holding warmth, a
miniature solar panel:

What engineering, tucked
in nature's soft folds,
design unmirrored:

And I, observer, tethered
to this moment: fleeting
   yet achingly full:

From this, the day rolls:
shared laughter, cracking
lobster tails, toasting:

Glass clinks, echoes of
friendship: we gather,
   rich in our simplicity:

Here, joy multiplies,
like sunlight in
   feathers, expanding in
our grasp:

We linger, our day sated
   with ordinary splendors,
content:

    Night falls, companions
depart: I am left with
warmth, gratitude:

Reflection on moments,
   small, large: how they
     build the edifice of
life:

Both fleeting and
eternal, the bird, the
meal, the laughter: all
  seeds, growing:

  Mud caked on boots, crisp
    air cuts—yet inside, a
      fire: thoughts stir:

Contrast: inner chaos,
outside, the world holds
its breath, still as a
frozen lake:

Silent: yet turmoil turns
within: my mind a flurry,
  snowstorm:

Caught between
    celebration, skepticism:
New Year's chimes, old
doubts resurface:

  In this quiet, a call:
embrace the new, yet hold
dear the known:

The bird knows not of
years, yet lives:
instinct its guide,
through seasons' swift
    change:

    And so must I navigate,
this dual course:
    cherishing simplicity,
probing depth:

The body complains,
   fatigue sets like frost,
   yet the mind wants to
   soar:

   Such contradictions are
we: bound yet unbounded,
earthed yet aspiring:

So I find solace, in the
smallest things: a bird
fluffs in sunlight:

And all is right, for a
   moment, as simple as
   warmth on wings.

Boundary Currents

In the confines of this
   narrow stream, each word:
a river stone settled in
silt, smoothed by the
constant rub of water,
     asserts itself against
    the flow: yet concedes to
the shapings of
    relentless currents.

The paradox of
 boundaries: how they
grant form to the
formless, yet chafe the
spirit that pushes
against their cool, hard
edges. These lines I lay
   down, like tracks on a
path that both guides and
     confines.

The tape rolls out, a
path clear but linear,
where the foot must
follow the foot, and the
eye leads the mind: could
it be that freedom finds
its breath in the
discipline of contours,
like the riverbank to the
river, a necessary
    imposition?

I think on this, typebars
    hovering over this
ribbon and paper: how much
    has escaped my note,
beyond capture, because I
    chose this narrow frame?
Does the frame define the
picture, or merely
isolate, part from part,
    the whole from the more?

Does a rule enhance, or
does it merely bind? The
tree grows skyward,
    straight: but also wide,
wild at the whim of wind
    and whimsy. Is there a
balance here, a midpoint
   where structure supports
and does not stifle?

Night comes, and the
    questions morph, as
shadows lengthen, into
doubts. My tape is full,
    yet empty, marked yet
    blank, definitive yet
unresolved. This paradox
is the crux of all
creation: where order
    meets the chaotic, where
form meets the formless,
where the line serves
   both to limit and to
  speak.

And so I must continue,
though each line could be
 an end, a wall, or a new
beginning. The page is
both open and closed, a
possibility defined by
its very limitations.

And tomorrow, as today, I
will roll out my tape
again, measuring
thoughts, not in breadth,
but depth: seeking that
point where constraint
becomes a conduit, where
the channel deepens the
flow rather than narrows
it.

Each line a paradox:
freedom within form, a
 silent music played on
the quiet fields of
 paper, where the white
 spaces speak as loudly as
the ink, and the margins,
hold the center.

Here, at the edge of
sleep, I acknowledge:
what is unfinished will
remain so, a testament to
 the process, not the
completion. For even as I

wrestle with the form,
the form whispers back, a
dialogue continuous as
breath, as elusive and
essential as the shape of
water flowing, forever
seeking, forever escaping
the confines of
definition.

And in this uneasy
acceptance, I find a kind
of peace: the artist must
    dance with canvas, and
the composer with the
scale, each finding
   freedom within the frame
of their craft.

So too does the poet need
   his tape: to draw the
line that both defines
and defies, to trace the
   path that walks the edge
of paradox, where every
boundary is both a
  beginning and an end. A
tension held, a balance
   poised: the beauty found
  within the contradiction,
   where the limit itself
  expands the field of the
infinite, stretching
beyond the horizon of the
   page.

Rain's Philosophy

Rain begins its fall:
soft, then gaining,
  patter on leaf and tin,
drumming a rhythm slowly,
then all at once, like
thoughts rushing in to
  fill the quiet.

It's a gentle coercion,
  the way water takes
command of the landscape,
molding soil, eroding
    rock, never forceful, yet
undeniably persistent:

Each drop a whisper,
nature's dialect. They
gather, speak in volumes,
flood the air with the
scent of wet earth.

I think of impermanence,
    how easily rain erases
footprints, leaving the
  path smoothed, renewed,
    in its ephemeral embrace.

The contrast sharpens: my
intellect eager to
  analyze each detail, each
interaction of droplet
and dust, while my senses

    urge surrender to the
enveloping mist.

Edges of thought blur
like the boundaries
between rain and river,
each drop untraceable,
    merging, becoming part of
something flowing and
    vast.

  Why do I strive to
    define, to understand,
when all around me is
flux, a continual dance
of forming and fading?

  The rain does not pause
for analysis, does not
categorize its own
descension, it simply
falls, exists,
transforms.

  And here I stand:
  conflicted, caught in the
downpour, wishing to
    simply be, to feel each
cool whisper of water, to
let it cleanse and carry
  away my cluttered
thoughts.

Leaves glisten, streets
 gleam, aware of nothing
but their wetness, their
part in this cycle of
refresh and renew.

 If I could dissolve like
salt in this ever-moving
 stream, lose myself to
 the rhythm of nature,
perhaps then, I could
 find peace, a silent
accord with the eternal
ebb and flow.

Perhaps it is not for us
to hold, to keep, to fix
in place— everything is
fleeting, and we, mere
observers of the vast
unfolding.

There's humility in the
rain, a lesson in each
 drop: that all we are,
all we have, is
temporary, washed away
with surprising
 gentleness.

Soon, the rain lessens,
drops sparse like the
 final words of a
concluding chapter.

The world is quiet,
softened, as if all
sharpness has been
smoothed away, as if
nothing remains but the
purity of the moment.

A quiet surrender: I let
　the rainfall, the fading
light, wash away my
concerns, my need for
　　　answers.

In the dimming day, I
find my clarity not in
　　the pursuit of knowledge,
　　but in the acceptance of
simple existence, the
falling rain the perfect
metaphor for the beauty
　of what simply is.

This evening, as darkness
gathers, rain's last
　whispers invite me to
rest, to dissolve my
fears in the quietude
they leave behind.

　Nothing remains but the
soft echo of rain, a
gentle reminder of life's
continuous flow, and my
　　　place within its

infinite, ever-changing
    tide.

Condensation's Philosophy

Drips fall: steady, slow,
the freeze melts into
flow, how simple this
   shift from solid to gift:

water, in beads, slides
down bark, the tree
    abides its roots, soaked,
unseen, drink deep;
nothing's lean.

Ice shards thin on rock,
    beneath, the stir of
stock, microbes wake from
chill, the earth's soft,
thrumming will.

  A leaf, cupped, now bears
  a pool: sky, distilled,
  it shares reflection,
ripple, merge: an urge,
to surge.

    Simple physics, this, or
   something missed in the
hiss of thought, the
   crawl of doubt: the
small.

   Might it be that sight is
as deep as night, that
  seeing folds in meaning,
thin?

A philosopher's dream— to
  glean beneath the seam.
Yet here: just water,
ice, and latter.

Condensing air, breath on
    cold glass: life meets
death, cycles spun close,
intimate: almost.

Does understanding deepen
    or simply leap in where
   observation dares to
stare?

The sky grays, evening
pulls its blanket,
 leaving drops that slow,
pace themselves, know.

Is there sense in asking,
or task in unmasking the
layers of plain truth:
rain?

   The season speaks less,
yet in its compress,
finds space enough for
ponder, the core.

Birds flit, pause, dip in
puddles, their sip a
ritual of survival:
   revival.

   Branches bear the weight,
of water, fate a pattern,
a call to fall.

And so, hours pass, one
drop amasses into
another, the blend—
begin, end.

 No need for the mind to
wind around the kind of
   questions that stall: the
      fall.

How natural to observe,
not to swerve into the
maze of why, simply
     comply.

   Trees know no concern,
their turn to return to
earth is but another
phase, no bother.

Here in the hush, no
rush, the world keeps its
weave, I perceive.

And what of the poet?
Does he show it— the way
nature sifts, lifts?

    Or does he overlay, with
words, the day? His
thoughts, perhaps, simply
traps.

As twilight eases, the
heart releases, there, in
the quiet, a diet.

Of simple things, the
 rings of drop, splash,
echo: let go.

    Water, the teacher,
gentle preacher, says:
behold, not more, the
pour.

The lessons of less,
compress, reveal in their
spare the bare.

A thought concludes,
intrudes no more than
necessary: the very
ordinary.

Yet in this minimal, the
primal feels immense,
  dense.

And I, watcher, learn to
turn from being actor to
reactor.

  The day's end, a slow
dimming, I know: it's
  enough to watch, not
botch.

  With a sense of peace, I
  cease, more observer than
server.

And in the minimal, find
the pinnacle of
existence: resistance is
distance.

  So let the cold night
hold tight, the water has
taught, sought.

Its lesson wrought in
simplicity, its thin veil
    a curtain, certain.

And behind it, nothing
more than the buffering
    of nature at play, day by
day.

Linguistic Topography

    Where words weave:
through the thicket and
thrum: the old tongues
twist, turning: like
    rivers cutting through
the stone-heart:
landscape, shaping

what we see: and
    therefore what we are,
changelings: in a wood of
    phrases, Danish
diphthongs and runic
rows: puzzle, pretzeled
syntax: my toy, my trial,

this bending of branches:
    that once bore straight
fruit, where now nuts
    gnarled and knotted:
fall, throwing off eater
and eater's path alike:

    do we speak: or are
spoken, language a leash:
    or a leaping point,
    etymology's roots running
deep: and dark, digging
    into damp: earth's
embrace,

    my thought's fabric
frays: at the pull of
ancient and futuristic,
tense: muddied as a
spring-runoff rivulet,
choked with the tongues:
of ten

thousand forebears, their
fibrous, silenced
    speeches: still sounding,
subterranean, seeping up
into: syntax, our daily
    spade and spoon,

could it be: our spate,
our specter, the ghost in
our machine: grinding
gears against the grain
    of modernity: making,
molding us, more than we
mold it,

a line laid out: with old
  world orders, obscures,
clears the path: both,
  bent back upon itself: a
branch broken under the
  weight: of its winter
snow,

much less straight: much
    more mystery, cleaved
clef: a note held over,

from a song long
  silenced: yet, resonating
still, in rings through

    this oak's old heartwood:
a language, a living: do
we shape it: or does it
shape us, the chisel: or
the wood,

is what we say: what we
  see, or do seams of
speech: stitch us into
    scenes unseen:
unthinking, until
unearthed by utterance,

 perhaps the play's the
thing: wherein we catch:
  the conscience of the
king, of ourselves, in
words wound: round,
rebound, how sound

the ground we think we
  stand: is it firm,
fashioned by fact, or do
    we dance on dialogues:
drifting, undirected, yet
deliberate: diction's
    drive,

this experiment:
linguistic, a lark,
perhaps, a leap: into the
unknown of our own
making, the muddle and
mix: of man's

monologue, not just with
others, but with the
self: 'self', even that a
word worn: from overuse,
understood or undermined:
by its

origins, the bones of
    language: lain bare, if
  but briefly, by playing:
with its body: breaking,
bonding again, how
mutable: the mortar

that holds our verbal
  bricks: together, the
    wall writes itself: while
  we but wonder, are we
builders: or built, the
syntax suppliers: or
supplied,

now, nearing the nerve:
    the quick, of this quaint
linguistic quest: if
words shape the world:
how much of our world is
  given: not gotten,

how much of what we
perceive: persists,
independent of the ink: I
spill, or the sounds I
send: spiraling into
ears, unfolding in minds:
  not mine,

if I change the way:
    these winds wind, will
the weather itself:
    alter, if I speak in
ancient accents: am I
heard differently, more
    deeply: or

  dismissed as decorative,:
a divergence from the
direct, does this dance
  of diction dilute: or
    deepen, the meaning, made
more: by its

making strange, are we
alien: in our own
    articulations, strangers:
to our selves, shaped by
sounds: so subtly, they
seem to stream: from our
souls,

    yet, are we the source:
or merely the vessel:
  through which ancient

streams still surge and
sing, carrying forward
echoes: of a thousand
tongues, shaping what
we think we shape.

Eternal Cycles

The morning breaks:
    crisp, cool: I greet its
pale light, flinching at
the chill that seeps into
my bones: fragile as thin
   ice on a freshly-frozen
pond.

Each breath puffs into
  mist, a vanishing act:
    coldproof of life's
temporary heat, of
essence held and
released: like words on a
frosted pane.

Trees stand: stark
   against the sky, their
  bark dark, cracked,
enduring: time's slow
etchings marking eternal
  cycles: seen but seldom
felt in fleeting flesh.

Leaves have abandoned
their posts, littering
the ground: depths of
decay that nourish new
  life: so all endings feed
beginnings in silent,
    sacred rhythm.

Walking, my steps crunch
against the frosted
grass: a sound like the
ticking of nature's
clock: relentless, yet
  comforting: the known
cadence of changing.

Philosopher minds debate
the mechanics of motion,
yet the planet spins not
a bit slower for
  pondering, nor does the
  cosmos pause for

  our human hesitations.
Look: the sun arcs in
sheer scope, regardless
  of witnesses, lights the
short days, lengthening
shadows cast by simple
truths.

I wonder: what binds this
  all— the spin, the light,
the shadow? And in the
  asking, lose thread of
thought, as a cloud
covers the sun: fleeting
eclipse.

Within these movements,
grand and minute, where
do my musings fit? Do

they ripple through the
air, stir the branches,
    shift the clouds, or
dissipate, unheard,
unseen?

Passing by a small brook,
its waters clear, cold,
and rushing: a mirror for
sky and leaf, and for the
fleeting thoughts like
  leaves that float upon
its surface.

    Each reflection—a story,
distorted by the water's
    flow, altered but based
    in truth: life's flowing
narrative, writ in water,
not set in stone.

  Days, like water, slip
past: soft, incessant:
carving canyons in the
landscape of our lives,
leaving us to ponder
depths unseen from the
surface's calm.

  How to measure such a
   span? Not in hours but in
changes, not by clocks
but by the hues of skies,
moods, and seasons: vast,

or in the pulse beneath
    skin.

And as this project ends,
I am caught in the
undertow of time's river,
knowing well each moment
passed is another gained,
   yet mourned for its
passing.

All things—this poem,
    winter's breath, my
transient thoughts—must
fade, succumb to the
   sweep of days, to the
   grand dissolve: quiet, as
snow settling on warm
    ground.

In this acceptance, a
   peace: not resignation
but a rich harvest of
moments lived and
observed, held close then
released into the flow
   from which they came.

What remains as my typewriter
stills? A canvas marked
by fleeting impressions,
an attempt to capture the
   uncapturable: life, too
vast for simple lines.

Yet within these limits,
a structure: necessary,
like banks that guide a
river's course. Without
    them, would these
       thoughts spill over, lost
in the terrain?

Perhaps. But here, now,
they are collected:
droplets in a stream,
making their way to join
a greater body, the whole
greater for their small
    presence.

And so, with a final
tap, I push away from my
typewriter, step back: the
landscape of ink and
thought completed, yet
   always just beginning, as
time ticks on.

In the cycle of creation,
the end is a new start:

www.ingramcontent.com/pod-product-compliance
Lightning Source LLC
Chambersburg PA
CBHW031644040426
42453CB00006B/201